Delights & Shadows

DELIGHTS & SHADOWS

poems by

TED KOOSER

COPPER CANYON PRESS

ACKNOWLEDGMENTS

We are grateful to the editors of the publications where some of these poems first appeared:

Acre, The Atlantic Monthly, Blink, The Chattahoochee Review, Connecticut Review, Field, Flyway, The Georgia Review, Great River Review, The Kenyon Review, Laurel Review, Margie, Metre, Nebraska Poets Calendar, North Dakota Quarterly, Northwest Florida Review, The Ohio Review, Plainsong, Poetry, Prairie Schooner, River Styx, Rosebud, Shenandoah, Solo, Southern Poetry Review, The Southern Review, Spirituality and Health, Third Coast, and *West Branch*

Cover art: George C. Ault, *August Night at Russell's Corners,* courtesy Joslyn Art Museum, Omaha, Nebraska; and Martha Parrish & James Reinish, Inc.

Copper Canyon Press is in residence under the auspices of the Centrum Foundation at Fort Worden State Park in Port Townsend, Washington. Centrum sponsors artist residencies, education workshops for Washington State students and teachers, Blues, Jazz, and Fiddle Tunes festivals, classical music performances, and the Port Townsend Writers' Conference.

LIBRARY OF CONGRESS CATALOGING-IN-PUBLICATION DATA

Kooser, Ted.
Delights and shadows: by Ted Kooser. — 1st ed.
    p. cm.
ISBN 1-55659-201-9 (alk. paper)
1. Title.
PS3561.O6D45 2004
811'.54 — DC22

                                                2003018447

9 8 7

COPPER CANYON PRESS
Post Office Box 271, Port Townsend, Washington 98368
www.coppercanyonpress.org

for Kathleen

The Sailor cannot see the North,
but knows the Needle can.

EMILY DICKINSON, IN A LETTER TO
THOMAS WENTWORTH HIGGINSON, 1862

Contents

III. BANK FISHING FOR BLUEGILLS

IV. THAT WAS I

Delights & Shadows

I. WALKING ON TIPTOE

Walking on Tiptoe

Long ago we quit lifting our heels
like the others—horse, dog, and tiger—
though we thrill to their speed
as they flee. Even the mouse
bearing the great weight of a nugget
of dog food is enviably graceful.
There is little spring to our walk,
we are so burdened with responsibility,
all of the disciplinary actions
that have fallen to us, the punishments,
the killings, and all with our feet
bound stiff in the skins of the conquered.
But sometimes, in the early hours,
we can feel what it must have been like
to be one of them, up on our toes,
stealing past doors where others are sleeping,
and suddenly able to see in the dark.

Tattoo

What once was meant to be a statement—
a dripping dagger held in the fist
of a shuddering heart—is now just a bruise
on a bony old shoulder, the spot
where vanity once punched him hard
and the ache lingered on. He looks like
someone you had to reckon with,
strong as a stallion, fast and ornery,
but on this chilly morning, as he walks
between the tables at a yard sale
with the sleeves of his tight black T-shirt
rolled up to show us who he was,
he is only another old man, picking up
broken tools and putting them back,
his heart gone soft and blue with stories.

At the Cancer Clinic

She is being helped toward the open door
that leads to the examining rooms
by two young women I take to be her sisters.
Each bends to the weight of an arm
and steps with the straight, tough bearing
of courage. At what must seem to be
a great distance, a nurse holds the door,
smiling and calling encouragement.
How patient she is in the crisp white sails
of her clothes. The sick woman
peers from under her funny knit cap
to watch each foot swing scuffing forward
and take its turn under her weight.
There is no restlessness or impatience
or anger anywhere in sight. Grace
fills the clean mold of this moment
and all the shuffling magazines grow still.

Student

The green shell of his backpack makes him lean
into wave after wave of responsibility,
and he swings his stiff arms and cupped hands,

paddling ahead. He has extended his neck
to its full length, and his chin, hard as a beak,
breaks the cold surf. He's got his baseball cap on

backward as up he crawls, out of the froth
of a hangover and onto the sand of the future,
and lumbers, heavy with hope, into the library.

Gyroscope

I place this within the first order
of wonders: a ten-year-old girl
alone on a sunny, glassed-in porch
in February, the world beyond
the windows slowly tipping forward
into spring, her thin arms held out
in the sleepwalker pose, and pinched
and stretched between her fingers,
a length of common grocery twine
upon which smoothly spins and leans
one of the smaller worlds we each
at one time learn to master, the last
to balance so lightly in our hands.

New Cap

Brown corduroy,
the earflaps tied on top,
the same size cap he bought
when he was young,
but at eighty-six
a head's a smaller thing,
the hair gone fine and thin,
less meat to the scalp,
and not so much
ambition packed inside.
He squints from under the bill
as if the world
were a long ways off,
and when he tips it back
to open up his face
to conversation,
it looks so loose
you think that one of them,
the cap or he,
might blow away.

Cosmetics Department

A fragrance heavy as dust, and two young women
motionless as mannequins, dressed in black.

The white moth of timelessness flutters about them,
unable to leave the cool light of their faces.

One holds the other's head in her hands
like a mirror. The other leans into the long fingers

knowing how heavy her beauty is. Eye to eye,
breath into breath, they lean as if frozen forever:

a white cup with two lithe figures painted in black
and the warm wine brimming.

Biker

Pulling away from a stoplight
with a tire's sharp bark,
he lifts his scuffed boot and kicks at the air,
and the old dog of inertia gets up with a growl
and shrinks out of the way.

The Old People

Pantcuffs rolled, and in old shoes,
they stumble over the rocks and wade out
into a cold river of shadows
far from the fire, so far that its warmth
no longer reaches them. And its light
(but for the sparks in their eyes
when they chance to look back)
scarcely brushes their faces. Their ears
are full of night: rustle of black leaves
against a starless sky. Sometimes
they hear us calling, and sometimes
they don't. They are not searching
for anything much, nor are they much
in need of finding something new.
They are feeling their way out into the night,
letting their eyes adjust to the future.

In January

Only one cell in the frozen hive of night
is lit, or so it seems:
this Vietnamese café, with its oily light,
its odors whose shapes are like flowers.
Laughter and talk, the tick of chopsticks.
Beyond the glass, the wintry city
creaks like an ancient wooden bridge.
A great wind rushes under all of us.
The bigger the window, the more it trembles.

A Rainy Morning

A young woman in a wheelchair,
wearing a black nylon poncho spattered with rain,
is pushing herself through the morning.
You have seen how pianists
sometimes bend forward to strike the keys,
then lift their hands, draw back to rest,
then lean again to strike just as the chord fades.
Such is the way this woman
strikes at the wheels, then lifts her long white fingers,
letting them float, then bends again to strike
just as the chair slows, as if into a silence.
So expertly she plays the chords
of this difficult music she has mastered,
her wet face beautiful in its concentration,
while the wind turns the pages of rain.

Mourners

After the funeral, the mourners gather
under the rustling churchyard maples
and talk softly, like clusters of leaves.
White shirt cuffs and collars flash in the shade:
highlights on deep green water.
They came this afternoon to say goodbye,
but now they keep saying hello and hello,
peering into each other's faces,
slow to let go of each other's hands.

Skater

She was all in black but for a yellow ponytail
that trailed from her cap, and bright blue gloves
that she held out wide, the feathery fingers spread,
as surely she stepped, click-clack, onto the frozen
top of the world. And there, with a clatter of blades,
she began to braid a loose path that broadened
into a meadow of curls. Across the ice she swooped
and then turned back and, halfway, bent her legs
and leapt into the air the way a crane leaps, blue gloves
lifting her lightly, and turned a snappy half-turn
there in the wind before coming down, arms wide,
skating backward right out of that moment, smiling back
at the woman she'd been just an instant before.

II. THE CHINA PAINTERS

The China Painters

They have set aside their black tin boxes,
scratched and dented,
spattered with drops of pink and blue;
and their dried-up, rolled-up tubes
of alizarin crimson, chrome green,
zinc white, and ultramarine;
their vials half full of gold powder;
stubs of wax pencils;
frayed brushes with tooth-bitten shafts;
and have gone in fashion and with grace
into the clouds of loose, lush roses,
narcissus, pansies, columbine,
on teapots, chocolate pots,
saucers and cups, the good Haviland dishes
spread like a garden
on the white lace Sunday cloth,
as if their souls were bees
and the world had been nothing but flowers.

Memory

Spinning up dust and cornshucks
as it crossed the chalky, exhausted fields,
it sucked up into its heart
hot work, cold work, lunch buckets,
good horses, bad horses, their names
and the names of mules that were
better or worse than the horses,
then rattled the dented tin sides
of the threshing machine, shook
the manure spreader, cranked
the tractor's crank that broke
the uncle's arm, then swept on
through the windbreak, taking
the treehouse and dirty magazines,
turning its fury on the barn
where cows kicked over buckets
and the gray cat sat for a squirt
of thick milk in its whiskers, crossed
the chicken pen, undid the hook,
plucked a warm brown egg
from the meanest hen, then turned
toward the house, where threshers
were having dinner, peeled back
the roof and the kitchen ceiling,
reached down and snatched up

uncles and cousins, grandma, grandpa,
parents and children one by one,
held them like dolls, looked
long and longingly into their faces,
then set them back in their chairs
with blue and white platters of chicken
and ham and mashed potatoes
still steaming before them, with
boats of gravy and bowls of peas
and three kinds of pie, and suddenly,
with a sound like a sigh, drew up
its crowded, roaring, dusty funnel,
and there at its tip was the nib of a pen.

Ice Cave

That hill's hard core of yellow stone held steady at 43 degrees
all year round, just warm enough in winter to work in
    shirtsleeves
stacking the milky slabs of ice sawed from the lid of the river
and sledged uphill with horses, then blanketed with sawdust
to hold the cold, to keep the past from trickling into
    the present.

In summer, it was a pleasant place to set up chairs and sit
    and talk,
the family together, the cool breath of the cave at their backs,
as they looked down over the roofs of farmhouse, barn, and
    pig shed,
down on the brown and steaming river, maybe chipping a
    piece of ice
from last year's winter to cool their lips, gone dry from stories.

Then dusk would come, and shadows stepped from behind
    the trees
and started uphill, and it seemed the cave would breathe a
    little cold
back into the darkening valley whence all cold would come,
and brushing sawdust from their arms, carrying their
    kitchen chairs,
they'd walk downhill, stiff-legged from sitting, hungry
    for supper.

Mother

Mid April already, and the wild plums
bloom at the roadside, a lacy white
against the exuberant, jubilant green
of new grass and the dusty, fading black
of burned-out ditches. No leaves, not yet,
only the delicate, star-petaled
blossoms, sweet with their timeless perfume.

You have been gone a month today
and have missed three rains and one nightlong
watch for tornadoes. I sat in the cellar
from six to eight while fat spring clouds
went somersaulting, rumbling east. Then it poured,
a storm that walked on legs of lightning,
dragging its shaggy belly over the fields.

The meadowlarks are back, and the finches
are turning from green to gold. Those same
two geese have come to the pond again this year,
honking in over the trees and splashing down.
They never nest, but stay a week or two
then leave. The peonies are up, the red sprouts
burning in circles like birthday candles,

for this is the month of my birth, as you know,
the best month to be born in, thanks to you,
everything ready to burst with living.
There will be no more new flannel nightshirts
sewn on your old black Singer, no birthday card
addressed in a shaky but businesslike hand.
You asked me if I would be sad when it happened

and I am sad. But the iris I moved from your house
now hold in the dusty dry fists of their roots
green knives and forks as if waiting for dinner,
as if spring were a feast. I thank you for that.
Were it not for the way you taught me to look
at the world, to see the life at play in everything,
I would have to be lonely forever.

A Jar of Buttons

This is a core sample
from the floor of the Sea of Mending,

a cylinder packed with shells
that over many years

sank through fathoms of shirts —
pearl buttons, blue buttons —

and settled together
beneath waves of perseverance,

an ocean upon which
generations of women set forth,

under the sails of gingham curtains,
and, seated side by side

on decks sometimes salted by tears,
made small but important repairs.

Dishwater

Slap of the screen door, flat knock
of my grandmother's boxy black shoes
on the wooden stoop, the hush and sweep
of her knob-kneed, cotton-aproned stride
out to the edge and then, toed in
with a furious twist and heave,
a bridge that leaps from her hot red hands
and hangs there shining for fifty years
over the mystified chickens,
over the swaying nettles, the ragweed,
the clay slope down to the creek,
over the redwing blackbirds in the tops
of the willows, a glorious rainbow
with an empty dishpan swinging at one end.

Depression Glass

It seemed those rose-pink dishes
she kept for special company
were always cold, brought down
from the shelf in jingling stacks,
the plates like the panes of ice
she broke from the water bucket
winter mornings, the flaring cups
like tulips that opened too early
and got bitten by frost. They chilled
the coffee no matter how quickly
you drank, while a heavy
everyday mug would have kept
a splash hot for the better
part of a conversation. It was hard
to hold up your end of the gossip
with your coffee cold, but it was
a special occasion, just the same,
to sit at her kitchen table
and sip the bitter percolation
of the past week's rumors from cups
it had taken a year to collect
at the grocery, with one piece free
for each five pounds of flour.

Zenith

It was part of her parlor's darkness
during the war years—its Gothic cabinet,
its shadowy speaker behind a thin lattice
like the face of a priest—but when
my grandmother snapped its switch
each evening to tune in the news,
it opened the tiny Japanese fan
of its dial and light spilled over her fingers,
swollen and stiff. And in near darkness
my sister and I, shushed into silence,
and Grandmother, rubbing and kneading
the pain from her hands, sat there
at the rear of the action, a patrol
in the weak yellow glow from the war.

The Necktie

His hands fluttered like birds,
each with a fancy silk ribbon
to weave into their nest,
as he stood at the mirror
dressing for work, waving hello
to himself with both hands.

Applesauce

I liked how the starry blue lid
of that saucepan lifted and puffed,
then settled back on a thin
hotpad of steam, and the way
her kitchen filled with the warm,
wet breath of apples, as if all
the apples were talking at once,
as if they'd come cold and sour
from chores in the orchard,
and were trying to shoulder in
close to the fire. She was too busy
to put in her two cents' worth
talking to apples. Squeezing
her dentures with wrinkly lips,
she had to jingle and stack
the bright brass coins of the lids
and thoughtfully count out
the red rubber rings, then hold
each jar, to see if it was clean,
to a window that looked out
through her back yard into Iowa.
And with every third or fourth jar
she wiped steam from her glasses,
using the hem of her apron,
printed with tiny red sailboats

that dipped along with leaf-green
banners snapping, under puffs
of pale applesauce clouds
scented with cinnamon and cloves,
the only boats under sail
for at least two thousand miles.

Creamed Corn

The Jamaicans who came to can corn
at the Green Giant plant in the '40s
were sinuously thin and so black
that a lame word offered to them in greeting
went right through their skins without
raising a ripple. Our own black families
(we spoke that way, of *our* black families),
the Martins and Shipps, had lived among us
so long it no longer mattered,
but these Jamaicans were different.
They kept to themselves, in loose clusters,
and knives flashed from the shadows
when they picked their teeth or scraped
Iowa from under their pale, perfect nails.
And when they talked they sounded like pianos;
all over the keyboard went their honky-tonk
laughing and talking. Word got around
that out of pure spite and meanness
sometimes they peed in the creamed corn
as it sluffed through the trough. Then the plant
shut down for the year, and they were gone,
and neighborly old Bob Martin rose up
and went down, up and down, in his place,
running the lift in our only hotel. Years later,
wherever we've gone, whatever we've come to,
our ignorance spoils the creamed corn.

Flow Blue China

No real flowers would give of themselves
as these do, the soft tips of their petals
easing out under the painted gold borders,
then bleeding into puffs of blue, and the aunt
who in her old age gave me these cups
and saucers, the plates, bread plates and platters,
the gravy boat, and the big covered bowl
that for seventy years she brought to her table
heaped high with buttercup potatoes,
she too, like one of these soft blue flowers,
has slipped beyond the thin line at the edge.
I lift this cup to her. Flow, blue.

Father

May 19, 1999

Today you would be ninety-seven
if you had lived, and we would all be
miserable, you and your children,
driving from clinic to clinic,
an ancient, fearful hypochondriac
and his fretful son and daughter,
asking directions, trying to read
the complicated, fading map of cures.
But with your dignity intact
you have been gone for twenty years,
and I am glad for all of us, although
I miss you every day—the heartbeat
under your necktie, the hand cupped
on the back of my neck, Old Spice
in the air, your voice delighted with stories.
On this day each year you loved to relate
that at the moment of your birth
your mother glanced out the window
and saw lilacs in bloom. Well, today
lilacs are blooming in side yards
all over Iowa, still welcoming you.

Pearl

Elkader, Iowa, a morning in March,
the Turkey River running brown and wrinkly
from a late spring snow in Minnesota,
a white two-story house on Mulberry Street,
windows flashing with sun, and I had come
a hundred miles to tell our cousin, Pearl,
that her childhood playmate, Vera, my mother,
had died. I knocked and knocked at the door
with its lace-covered oval of glass, and at last
she came from the shadows and with one finger
hooked the curtain aside, peered into my face
through her spectacles, and held that pose,
a grainy family photograph that could have been
that of her mother. I called out, "Pearl,
it's Ted. It's Vera's boy," and my voice broke,
for it came to me, nearly sixty, I was still
my mother's boy, that boy for the rest of my life.

Pearl, at ninety, was one year older than Mother
and a widow for twenty years. She wore
a pale blue cardigan buttoned over a housedress,
and she shook my hand in the tentative way
of old women who rarely have hands to shake.
When I told her that Mother was gone, that she'd
died the evening before, she said she was sorry,

that "Vera wrote me a letter a while ago
to say she wasn't good." We went to the kitchen
and I sat at the table while she heated a pan
of water and made us cups of instant coffee.
She told me of a time when the two of them
were girls and crawled out onto the porch roof
to spy on my Aunt Mabel and a suitor
who were swinging below. "We got so excited
we had to pee, and we couldn't wait, and peed
right there on the roof and it trickled down
over the edge and dripped in the bushes,
but Mabel and that fellow never heard!"

We took our cups into her living room,
where stripes from the drawn blinds draped over
the World's Fair satin pillows. She took the couch
and I took a chair across from her. "I've had
some trouble with health myself," she said,
taking off her glasses and wiping them,
and I said she looked good, though, and she said,
"I've started seeing people who aren't here.
I know they're not real but I see them the same.
They come in the house and sit around
and never say a word. They keep their heads down
or cover their faces with cloths. I'm not afraid,

but I don't know what they want of me.
You won't be able to see, but one's right there
on the staircase where the light falls through
that window, a man in a light gray outfit."
I turned to look at the landing, where a patch
of light fell over the carpeted steps.
"Sometimes I think that my Max is with them;
one seems to know his way around the house.
What bothers me, Ted, is that they've started
to write out lists of everything I own.
They go from room to room, three or four
at a time, picking up things and putting them back.
I've talked to Wilson, the chiropractor,
and he just says that maybe it's time for me
to go to the nursing home." I asked her
what her regular doctor said and she said
she didn't go there anymore, that "He's
not much good." "But surely there's medicine,"
I said, and she said, "Maybe so." And then
there was a pause that filled the room.

After a while we began to talk again,
of other things, and there were some stories
we laughed a little over, and I wept a little,
and then it was time for me to go, to drive

the long miles back, and she slowly walked me
to the door and took my hand again—
our warm bony hands among the light hands
of the shadows that reached to touch us but
drew back—and I cleared my throat and said
I hope she'd take care of herself, and think
about seeing a real medical doctor,
and she said she'd give some thought to that,
and I took my hand from hers and waved goodbye
and the door closed, and behind the lace
the others stepped out of the stripes of light
and resumed their inventory, touching
the spoon I used and subtracting it from
the sum of the spoons in the kitchen drawer.

Old Cemetery

Somebody has been here this morning
to cut the grass, coming and going unseen
but leaving tracks, probably driving a pickup
with a low mower trailer that bent down
the weeds in the lane from the highway,
somebody paid by the job, not paid enough,
and mean and peevish, too hurried
to pull the bindweed that weaves up
into the filigreed iron crosses
or to trim the tall red prairie grass
too close to the markers to mow
without risking the blade. Careless
and reckless, too, leaving green paint
scraped from the deck of the mower
on the cracked concrete base of a marker.
The dead must have been overjoyed
to have their world back to themselves,
to hear the creak of trailer springs
under the weight of the cooling mower
and to hear the pickup turn over and over
and start at last, and drive away,
and then to hear the soft ticking of weeds
springing back, undeterred, in the lane
that leads nowhere the dead want to go.

A Winter Morning

A farmhouse window far back from the highway
speaks to the darkness in a small, sure voice.
Against this stillness, only a kettle's whisper,
and against the starry cold, one small blue ring of flame.

III. BANK FISHING FOR BLUEGILLS

Bank Fishing for Bluegills

A breeze nudges the empty aluminum boat
as it drifts at the end of its rope,
its lightness wallowing within it like a fat man
who has fished all day and fallen asleep
and is dreaming of when he was a little boy
and weighed no more than a plastic bucket.
Years of floating alone, fishing far
from the tourist cabins shining like rivets
along the water's edge, have bleached the blue
from his overalls and denim shirt.
His face has the flat gray sheen of a man
with a failing heart, but he is all lightness now,
and tethered only gently to this world.

Four Civil War Paintings by Winslow Homer

...if the painter shows that he observes more than
he reflects, we will forget the limitation and take his
work as we take nature, which, if it does not think, is
yet the cause of thought in us.

The Evening Post, NEW YORK, MAY 31, 1865

1. SHARPSHOOTER

A Union sniper in a tree

Some part of art is the art
of waiting—the chord
behind the tight fence
of a musical staff,
the sonnet shut in a book.
This is a painting of
waiting: the sharp crack
of the rifle still coiled
under the tiny
percussion cap, the cap
poised under the cocked
curl of the hammer,
and this young man among
the pine needles,
his finger as light as a breath
on the trigger,

just a pinpoint of light
in his one open eye,
like a star you might see
in broad daylight,
if you thought to look up.

2. THE BRIGHT SIDE

Black Union teamsters at
rest against a yellow tent

Though they lie in the sun,
the light does not glance from
buckle or button, nor from
their shadowy faces or hands
(one faint highlight, like a twist
of cotton, on the bill of a cap).
Instead, the sun seems to soak
into their sweaty clothes
and their skin, making them
even more black than they were.
On the bright side of their tent
they look like a ragged hole,
they look like oily cannon rags
or a heap of old harness.
Beyond, mules graze on light,
and canvas-topped wagons
loom bright as sails, so airy
you would think they were
empty. Perhaps they are,
perhaps these five black men
have taken on all of the load,
the powder kegs, the bags
of potatoes, the canisters of lead,
so dark, so heavy is their sleep
(with one man left awake
to smoke his pipe and watch).

3. PRISONERS FROM THE FRONT

Three Confederate soldiers awaiting
their disposition by a Union general

The youngest captive wears full
butternut regalia, is handsome
with long red hair, his field cap
cocked, one hand on his hip, a man
not ready to be immortalized
under yellowing varnish. An old man
stands next in line, bearded
and wearing a ragged brown coat.
He slumps like the very meaning
of surrender, but his jaw is set
and his eyes are like flashes
from distant cannon (we have waited
a hundred and forty years
to hear those reports). The third
is hot and young and ornery,
wearing a floppy hat, brim up,
his military coat unbuttoned,
hands stuffed in his pockets,
his mouth poised to spit.
It would be he who would ruin
the Union general's moment,
this formal military portrait,
that neat blue uniform, the cavalry
saber and fancy black hat. He would
surely do something to spoil it
if the painter would give him the chance.

4. THE VETERAN IN A NEW FIELD

A lone man scything wheat

His back is turned to us, his white shirt
the brightest thing in the painting.
Old trousers, leather army suspenders.
Before him the red wheat bends,
the sky is cloudless, smokeless, and blue.
Where he has passed, the hot stalks spread
in streaks, like a shell exploding, but that is
behind him. With stiff, bony shoulders
he mows his way into the colors of summer.

Turkey Vultures

Circling above us, their wing-tips fanned
like fingers, it is as if they are smoothing

one of those tissue-paper sewing patterns
over the pale blue fabric of the air,

touching the heavens with leisurely pleasure,
just a word or two called back and forth,

taking all the time in the world, even though
the sun is low and red in the west, and they

have fallen behind with the making of shrouds.

Pegboard

It has been carefully painted
with the outlines of tools
to show us which belongs where,
auger and drawknife,
claw hammer and crosscut saw,
like the outlines of hands on the walls
of ancient caves in France,
painted with soot mixed with spit
ten thousand years ago
in the faltering firelight of time,
hands borrowed to work on the world
and never returned.

At the County Museum

Blacker than black, the lacquered horse-drawn hearse,
dancing with stars from the overhead lights,

has clattered to a stop, but its waxy panels
are dusted each morning, as if it might be summoned

back into harness, to be hauled once again
through the wake of matched horses, the sweep

of their tails, its oak spokes soberly walking,
each placed squarely in front of the next

along pinstriped rims that carefully unreeled
hard ruts the wheels could follow home.

How many times must a thing like this be emptied
to look so empty? Its top like a table

from which a hundred years have been cleared,
and the crumbs brushed away, with nickel vases

at all four corners, set down after a toast
of fresh flowers has been offered and drained.

And on the board bench where dozens of drivers
jounced year into year, clicking their tongues,

is a black plush cushion that for each, for a time,
helped to soften the nearness of death.

Casting Reels

You find them at flea markets
and yard sales, old South Bends
and Pfluegers, with fancy engraving,
knurled knobs and pearl handles,
spooled with the fraying line
of long stories snarled into
silence, not just exaggerated tales
of walleyes, bass, and catfish,
but of hardworking men
who on Saturdays sought out
the solace of lakes, who on weekdays
at desks, or standing on ladders,
or next to clattering machines
played out their youth and strength
waiting to set the hook, and then,
in their sixties, felt the line go slack
and reeled the years back empty.
They are the ones who got away.

Horse

In its stall stands the 19th century,
its hide a hot shudder of satin,
head stony and willful,
an eye brown as a river and watchful:
a sentry a long way ahead
of a hard, dirty army of hooves.

Praying Hands

There is at least one pair
in every thrift shop in America,
molded in plastic or plaster of paris
and glued to a plaque,
or printed in church-pamphlet colors
and framed under glass.
Today I saw a pair made out of
lightweight wire stretched over a pattern
of finishing nails.
This is the way faith goes
from door to door,
cast out of one and welcomed at another.
A butterfly presses its wings like that
as it rests between flowers.

Lobocraspis griseifusa

This is the tiny moth who lives on tears,
who drinks like a deer at the gleaming pool
at the edge of the sleeper's eye, the touch
of its mouth as light as a cloud's reflection.

In your dream, a moonlit figure appears
at your bedside and touches your face.
He asks if he might share the poor bread
of your sorrow. You show him the table.

The two of you talk long into the night,
but by morning the words are forgotten.
You awaken serene, in a sunny room,
rubbing the dust of his wings from your eyes.

Home Medical Dictionary

This is not so much a dictionary
as it is an atlas for the old,
in which they pore over
the pink and gray maps of the body,
hoping to find that wayside junction
where a pain-rutted road
intersects with the highway
of answers, and where the slow river
of fear that achingly meanders
from organ to organ
is finally channeled and dammed.

In the Hall of Bones

Here we store the reassembled
scaffolding, the split, bleached uprights,
the knobby corner locks and braces
that held up the mastodon's
bag of wet leaves and the ivory
forklift of its head. Over there are
the planks upon which lay the turtle's
diving bell, and the articulated
rack that kept the dromedary's hump
from collapsing under the weight
of its perseverance. And here is
the basket that held the clip-clop
pulse of the miniature horse
as it dreamed of growing tall enough
to have lunch from a tree. And then
here's man, all matchsticks, wooden spoons,
and tongue depressors wired together,
a rack supporting a leaky jug
of lust and worry. Of all the skeletons
assembled here, this is the only one
in which once throbbed a heart
made sad by brooding on its shadow.

A Jacquard Shawl

A pattern of curly acanthus leaves,
and woven into one corner
in blue block letters half an inch tall:
MADE FROM WOOL FROM SHEEP
KILLED BY DOGS. 1778.
As it is with jacquards,
the design reverses to gray on blue
when you turn it over,
and the words run backward
into the past. The rest of the story
lies somewhere between one side
and the other, woven into
the plane where the colors reverse:
the circling dogs, the terrified sheep,
the meadow stippled with blood,
and the weaver by lamplight
feeding what wool she was able to save
into the faintly bleating, barking loom.

Telescope

This is the pipe that pierces the dam
that holds back the universe,

that takes off some of the pressure,
keeping the weight of the unknown

from breaking through
and washing us all down the valley.

Because of this small tube,
through which a cold light rushes

from the bottom of time,
the depth of the stars stays always constant

and we are able to sleep, at least for now,
beneath the straining wall of darkness.

A Box of Pastels

I once held on my knees a simple wooden box
in which a rainbow lay dusty and broken.
It was a set of pastels that had years before
belonged to the painter Mary Cassatt,
and all of the colors she'd used in her work
lay open before me. Those hues she'd most used,
the peaches and pinks, were worn down to stubs,
while the cool colors—violet, ultramarine—
had been set, scarcely touched, to one side.
She'd had little patience with darkness, and her heart
held only a measure of shadow. I touched
the warm dust of those colors, her tools,
and left there with light on the tips of my fingers.

Old Lilacs

Through early April cold,
these thin gray horses
have come near the house
as to a fence, and lean there
hungry for summer,
nodding their heads
with a nickering of twigs.

Their long legs are dusty
from standing for months
in winter's stall, and their eyes
are like a cloudy sky
seen through bare branches.

They are waiting for May
to come up from the barn
with her overalls pockets
stuffed with the fodder
of green. In a month
they will be slow and heavy,
their little snorts so sweet
you'll want to stand
among them, breathing.

Grasshoppers

This year they are exactly the size
of the pencil stub my grandfather kept
to mark off the days since rain,

and precisely the color of dust, of the roads
leading back across the dying fields
into the '30s. Walking the cracked lane

past the empty barn, the empty silo,
you hear them tinkering with irony,
slapping the grass like drops of rain.

The Beaded Purse

for Keith Jacobshagen

Dressed in his church suit, and under
the shadow of his hat, the old man
stood on the wooden depot platform
three feet above the rest of Kansas
while the westbound train chuffed in
and hissed to a stop. He and the agent
and two men, commercial travelers
waiting to go on west, pulled mailbags
out of the steam, then slid out
his daughter's coffin, canvas over wood,
and set it on a nearby baggage cart.

Not till the train had rolled away
and tooted once as it passed the shacks
at the leading edge of the distance,
and not till the agent had disappeared,
dragging the bags of mail behind,
did the old man pry up the nailed-down lid
with a bar he'd brought in the wagon.

Hat in hand, he took a long look.
He hadn't seen her in a dozen years.
At nineteen, without his blessing,
she'd gone back east to be an actress,
now and then writing her mother
in a carefree, ne'er-do-well cursive
to say she was happy, living in style.

A week before, the agent sent word
that there was a telegram waiting,
and the old man and his wife rode to town
to read that their daughter had died
and her remains were on the way home.
Remains, that's how they put it.

She was wearing a fancy yellow dress
but was no longer young and pretty.
She looked like one of the worn-out dolls
she'd left in her room at the farm
where he would sometimes go to sit.

A bag of women's private underthings
had been stuffed between her feet,
and someone had pushed down next to her
an evening bag beaded with pearls.

He opened the purse and found it empty,
so he took a few bills out of his pocket
and folded them in, then snapped it closed
for her mother to find. Then, with the back
of the bar he tapped the lid in place
and went to find the station agent.

The two of them lifted the coffin down
and carried it a few hard yards across
the sunny, dusty floor of Kansas
and loaded it onto the creaking wagon.

Then, clapping his hat on his head
and slapping the plump rump of his mare
with the reins, he started the long haul home
with his rich and famous daughter.

IV. THAT WAS I

That Was I

I was that older man you saw sitting
in a confetti of yellow light and falling leaves
on a bench at the empty horseshoe courts
in Thayer, Nebraska—brown jacket, soft cap,
wiping my glasses. I had noticed, of course,
that the rows of sunken horseshoe pits
with their rusty stakes, grown over with grass,
were like old graves, but I was not letting
my thoughts go there. Instead I was looking
with hope to a grapevine draped over
a fence in a neighboring yard, and knowing
that I could hold on. Yes, that was I.

And that was I, the round-shouldered man
you saw that afternoon in Rising City
as you drove past the abandoned Mini Golf,
fists deep in my pockets, nose dripping,
my cap pulled down against the wind
as I walked the miniature Main Street
peering into the child-size plywood store,
the poor red school, the faded barn, thinking
that not even in such an abbreviated world
with no more than its little events—the snap
of a grasshopper's wing against a paper cup—
could a person control this life. Yes, that was I.

And that was I you spotted that evening
just before dark, in a weedy cemetery
west of Staplehurst, down on one knee
as if trying to make out the name on a stone,
some lonely old man, you thought, come there
to pity himself in the reliable sadness
of grass among graves, but that was not so.
Instead I had found in its perfect web
a handsome black and yellow spider
pumping its legs to try to shake my footing
as if I were a gift, an enormous moth
that it could snare and eat. Yes, that was I.

Screech Owl

All night each reedy whinny
from a bird no bigger than a heart
flies out of a tall black pine
and, in a breath, is taken away
by the stars. Yet, with small hope
from the center of darkness
it calls out again and again.

A Spiral Notebook

The bright wire rolls like a porpoise
in and out of the calm blue sea
of the cover, or perhaps like a sleeper
twisting in and out of his dreams,
for it could hold a record of dreams
if you wanted to buy it for that,
though it seems to be meant for
more serious work, with its
college-ruled lines and its cover
that states in emphatic white letters,
5 SUBJECT NOTEBOOK. It seems
a part of growing old is no longer
to have five subjects, each
demanding an equal share of attention,
set apart by brown cardboard dividers,
but instead to stand in a drugstore
and hang on to one subject
a little too long, like this notebook
you weigh in your hands, passing
your fingers over its surfaces
as if it were some kind of wonder.

The Early Bird

Still dark, and raining hard
on a cold May morning

and yet the early bird
is out there chirping,

chirping its sweet-sour
wooden-pulley notes,

pleased, it would seem,
to be given work,

hauling the heavy
bucket of dawn

up from the darkness,
note over note,

and letting us drink.

Starlight

All night, this soft rain from the distant past.
No wonder I sometimes waken as a child.

On the Road

By the toe of my boot,
a pebble of quartz,
one drop of the earth's milk,
dirty and cold.
I held it to the light
and could almost see through it
into the grand explanation.
Put it back, something told me,
put it back and keep walking.

A Washing of Hands

She turned on the tap and a silver braid
unraveled over her fingers.
She cupped them, weighing that tassel,
first in one hand and then the other,
then pinched through the threads
as if searching for something, perhaps
an entangled cocklebur of water,
or the seed of a lake. A time or two
she took the tassel in both hands,
squeezed it into a knot, wrung out
the cold and the light, and then, at the end,
pulled down hard on it twice,
as if the water were a rope and she was
ringing a bell to call me, two bright rings,
though I was there.

After Years

Today, from a distance, I saw you
walking away, and without a sound
the glittering face of a glacier
slid into the sea. An ancient oak
fell in the Cumberlands, holding only
a handful of leaves, and an old woman
scattering corn to her chickens looked up
for an instant. At the other side
of the galaxy, a star thirty-five times
the size of our own sun exploded
and vanished, leaving a small green spot
on the astronomer's retina
as he stood in the great open dome
of my heart with no one to tell.

Garage Sale

All of your husband's shirts and slacks
and heavy sweaters — a bank of threatening clouds
that hang from a pipe between two ladders —
are much too big for me, and his extra boots
look cold and deep as abandoned wells,
and his tools are no good to anyone but him:
the head of his hammer is loose from pounding,
and he has twisted his screwdriver out
of its handle, and burned through the cord
on his soldering iron and chipped up the blade
of his crosscut saw, and all with the fingers
he touches you with. Where can he be
while I chat with you about the rain, beginning
to ring the fenders of trikes and bikes
parked in ranks on the drive? Where is he
as you and I carry the table of baby clothes
back under your roof and the rain wets the down
on your freckled, elbowy arms and shines
on your face and small round hopeful shoulders?
I walk so empty-handed to my car.

Surviving

There are days when the fear of death
is as ubiquitous as light. It illuminates
everything. Without it, I might not
have noticed this ladybird beetle,
bright as a drop of blood
on the window's white sill.
Her head no bigger than a period,
her eyes like needle points,
she has stopped for a moment to rest,
knees locked, wing covers hiding
the delicate lace of her wings.
As the fear of death, so attentive
to everything living, comes near her,
the tiny antennae stop moving.

A Glimpse of the Eternal

Just now,
a sparrow lighted
on a pine bough
right outside
my bedroom window
and a puff
of yellow pollen
flew away.

Tectonics

In only a few months
there begin to be fissures
in what we remember,
and within a year or two,
the facts break apart
one from another
and slowly begin to shift
and turn, grinding,
pushing up over each other
until their shapes
have been changed
and the past has become
a new world.
And after many years,
even a love affair,
one lush green island
all to itself,
perfectly detailed
with even a candle
softly lighting a smile,
may slide under the waves
like Atlantis,
scarcely rippling the heart.

A Happy Birthday

This evening, I sat by an open window
and read till the light was gone and the book
was no more than a part of the darkness.
I could easily have switched on a lamp,
but I wanted to ride this day down into night,
to sit alone and smooth the unreadable page
with the pale gray ghost of my hand.

About the Author

Ted Kooser is the author of ten books of poems, including *Braided Creek: A Conversation in Poetry,* written in collaboration with Jim Harrison and published by Copper Canyon Press in 2003. His poetry and nonfiction have been awarded a number of literary prizes and distinctions, including two NEA fellowships in writing. He is a retired life insurance executive who lives on an acreage near the village of Garland, Nebraska.

The Chinese character for poetry is made up of two parts: "word" and
"temple." It also serves as pressmark for Copper Canyon Press.

Founded in 1972, Copper Canyon Press remains dedicated to
publishing poetry exclusively, from Nobel laureates to new and
emerging authors. The Press thrives with the generous patronage of
readers, writers, booksellers, librarians, teachers, students, and funders
—everyone who shares the conviction that poetry invigorates the
language and sharpens our appreciation of the world.

THE ALLEN FOUNDATION *for* THE ARTS

NATIONAL
ENDOWMENT
FOR THE ARTS

The Allen Foundation for The Arts
Lannan Foundation
National Endowment for the Arts
Washington State Arts Commission

The Board and Staff express
gratitude to CYNTHIA HARTWIG
for her years of generous dedication
to Copper Canyon Press.

For information and catalogs:

COPPER CANYON PRESS
Post Office Box 271
Port Townsend, Washington 98368
360/385-4925
www.coppercanyonpress.org

❧

This book is set in New Caledonia, designed by William A. Dwiggins in 1939 after the Scotch faces of the nineteenth century. Book design by Valerie Brewster, Scribe Typography. Printed on archival-quality Glatfelter Authors Text at McNaughton and Gunn, Inc.

❧